PAGES FROM A DIARY WRITTEN IN
NINETEEN HUNDRED AND THIRTY
BY WILLIAM BUTLER YEATS

THE CUALA PRESS
DUBLIN IRELAND
MCMXLIV

The word "verify" occurs twice in the Diary. The verifications have been made in the footnotes on pages 21 and 32. I have added a few other explanatory notes. The design on the Title Page is from a drawing by Edmund Dulac originally made for the first edition of "A Vision".

George Yeats.

I

Portofino Vetta April 7th.

I have been ill for five months since I bled from the lung in London, four out of the five of Malta fever, and a couple of weeks ago the doctor told me it would be three months before I had received strength. But eight days ago we came from Rapallo to this hotel at Portofino Vetta some fifteen feet above the sea and I am almost well again. I work at the new version of *The Vision* every morning, then read Swift's Letters and only take to detective stories in the evening, and would be wholly well if my legs were stronger. Here I can slip in and out as I please, free from the stage fright I had at Rapallo whenever George brought me to the little Café by the sea. After all there may be something in climate which I have always denied. Here no mountains shut us in; I think three weeks should make me well as ever.

II

I am reading Swift — his Letters, his essay on the end of Queen Anne's reign, and contrasting them with Oliver's *Great Adventure*.* Oliver, like all modern historians, sees history as a reasoned conflict of mechanical interests intelligible to all. I think of Swift's account of Marlborough's demand to be

* F. S. Oliver, "The Endless Adventure".

made general for life, of the Queen's fear that he had designs against the throne, of Argyll's boast that he would fetch him from the midst of his army dead or alive. These men sat next one another, suspected one another, and planned we do not know what. History seems to me a human drama, keeping the classical unities by the clear division of its epochs, turning one way or the other because this man hates or that man loves. Had any trade question at the opening of the eighteenth century as great an effect on subsequent history as Bolingbroke's impatience and Harley's slowness and secrecy? Was the French Revolution caused by the peasants' poverty or by that which used it? The peasant had been poor for centuries. Yet the drama has its plot, and this plot ordained character and passions and exists for their sake.

III

Subject for a poem. April 30th.
Death of a friend. To describe how mixed with one's grief comes the thought, that the witness of some foolish word or act of one's own is gone.
Describe Byzantium as it is in the system towards the end of the first Christian millenium. A walking mummy. Flames at the street corners where the soul is purified, birds of hammered gold singing in the golden trees, in the harbour, offering their backs

to the wailing dead that they may carry them to paradise.

These subjects have been in my head for some time, especially the last.

IV

The heart well worn upon the sleeve may be the
   best of sights,
But never, never dangling leave the liver and the
   lights.*

V

When my instructors began their exposition of the Great Year all the history I knew was what I remembered of English and Classical history from school days, or had since learned from the plays of Shakespeare or the novels of Dumas. When I had the dates and diagrams I began to study it, but could not so late in life, and with so much else to read, be a deep student. So there is little in what follows but what comes from the most obvious authorities. Sometimes I did indeed stray from them, and sometimes the more vivid the fact the less do I remember my authority. Where did I pick up that story of the Byzantine bishop and the singer of Antioch, where learn that to anoint your body with the fat of a lion ensured the favour of a king?

* On reading poems by certain young writers in an American magazine of verse.

VI

A Dream

I dreamed that I was on shipboard, steerage on a crowded steamer. A steward asked me for my ticket but I had none. As the steamer had started he left me without doing anything. Presently a small man I knew to be a pickpocket said: "I will protect you". Then a big man I knew to be a tramp called me over to the other side of the steamer and showed me a better seat than the one I was sitting on and said: "I will protect you". I saw a woman smiling and we fell into talk.

"I think you know who I am".

"I know Sligo".

"I am a stowaway, but a tramp and a pickpocket have promised to protect me".

"There are people everybody protects".

"Who?"

"Those who speak well of their wives".

But another woman said: "That is not true. Everybody protects those who praise everybody but there has to be wisdom in it".

VII

Struck by this in Swift's *Discourse of the Contests and Dissensions between the Nobles and Commons in Athens and Rome*. "I think that the saying 'Vox populi vox Dei' ought to be understood of the universal bent and current of a people, not of the bare majority of a few representatives, which is often procured by little art, and great industry and application; wherein those who engage in the pursuits of malice and revenge, are much more sedulous than such as would prevent them." Vol II page 408 of Sheridan's Swift.

The whole essay leads up to Burke so clearly that one may claim that Anglo-Ireland recreated conservative thought as much in one as in the other. Indeed the *Discourse* with its law of history might be for us what Vico is to the Italians, had we a thinking nation.

VIII

Burke is only tolerable in his impassioned moments, but no matter what Swift talks of one delights in his animation and clarity. I think the reason is that Swift always thought in English and is learned in that tongue. The writers who seem most characteristic of his time, Pope in his verse for instance, and the great orators, think in French or in Latin. How much of my reading is to discover the English and Irish originals of my thought, its first language, and, where no such originals exist, its relation to what original did. I seek more than idioms, for thoughts become more vivid when I find they were thought out in historical circumstances which affect those in which I live, or, which is perhaps the same thing, were thought first by men my ancestors may have known. Some of my ancestors may have seen Swift, and probably my Huguenot grandmother who asked burial near Bishop King, spoke both to Swift and Berkeley. I have before me an ideal expression in which all that I have, clay and spirit alike, assist; it is as though I most approximate towards that expression when I carry with me the greatest possible amount of hereditary thought and feeling, even national and family hatred and pride.

Our poetry and prose are often abstract and foreign. I am a poor French scholar, yet in old days I felt my sentences take a French form. Yet we must not put an artificial emphasis on what is English or Irish, for if we do we no longer find new richness. I think of that supreme ceremony wherein the Mormon offers his wisdom to his ancestors. But our language and thought are broken from the past by hurry, even when we do not think in any foreign tongue. I can hear Swift's voice in his letters speaking the sentences at whatever pace makes their sound and idiom expressive. He speaks and we listen at leisure.

Burke, whether he wrote a pamphlet or prepared a speech, wrote for men in an assembly, whereas Swift wrote for men sitting at table or fireside — from that comes his animation and his naturalness.

Upon the other hand the sense of an assembly, of an exceptional occasion, rouses Burke to his great moments of passion.

IX

Pound's conception of excellence, like that of all revolutionary schools, is of something so international that it is abstract and outside life. I do not ask myself whether what I find in Elizabethan English, or in that of the early eighteenth century, is better or worse than what I find in some other clime and time. I can only approach that more distant excellence through what I inherit, lest I find it and be stricken dumb. "As ye came from Walsinghame" — *The Lamentation for Matthew Henderson*, "For Matthew was a queer man" — that modern song of the man sailing from Mayo* — show hereditary stamina and a great voice. A good poet, Henley said of Burns, be the a great voice. A good poet must, as Henley said of Burns be the last of a dynasty, and he must see to it that his court expels the parvenu even though he gather all the riches of the world.

X

A poet whose free verse I have admired*[2] rejects God and every kind of unity, calls the ultimate reality anarchy, means by that word something which for

* F. R. Higgins. "The Ballad of O'Bruadir".
*2 Basil Bunting. "Redimiculum Matellarum." Milan 1930.

lack of metaphysical knowledge he cannot define. He thinks however that a baptismal and marriage service and some sort of ceremonial preparation for death are necessary, and that the churches should stick to these and be content.

He now writes in the traditional forms because they satisfy a similar need. But why stop at the metrical forms. It has always seemed to me that all great literature at its greatest intensity displays the sage, the lover, or some image of despair, and that these are traditional attitudes. When I say the lover I mean all that heroic casuistry, all that assertion of the eternity of what nature declares ephemeral; and when I speak of an image of despair I think of a passage in Sophocles, or many passages in Shakespeare and in the old Testament; and when I say the sage I think of something Asiatic, and of something that belongs to modern Europe — the Pedlar in *The Excursion*, an old Hermit in *The Well at the World's End*, passages in Matthew Arnold.

All three have collapsed in our day because writers have grown weary of the old European philosophy and found no other. I think of the passage from Bacon quoted by Wordsworth as a motto to *The White Doe of Rylstone*, God puts divinity into a man as a man puts humanity into his dog. When the image of despair departed with poetical tragedy the others could not survive, for the lover and the sage cannot survive without that despair which is a form of joy and has certainly no place in the modern psychological study of suffering. Does not the soldier become the sage, or should I have granted him a different category, when some Elizabethan tragedy makes him reply to a threat of hanging "What has that to do with me?"

I asked, when a lad of seventeen or eighteen, a learned Brahmin how he taught philosophy to a man who denied the soul's immortality. "I say to him" he said "What have you to do with that?" words which assert the soul's supremacy as do Hamlet's "Absent thee from felicity awhile" and all of Shakespeare's other last words and closing scenes.

I find among some of the newer school of poets hatred of every monotheistic system.

XI

Protestant Ireland should ask permission to bring back the body of Grattan from Westminster Abbey to St. Patrick's. He was buried in Westminster against the protests of his friends and followers — according to Sir Jonah Barrington, that there might be no place of pilgrimage — abandoned there without bust or monument. I would have him brought back through streets lined with soldiers that we might affirm that St. Patrick's is more to us than

Westminster; but, though Protestant Ireland should first move in this matter, I would have all descendants of Grattan's party or of those who voted against the Union, lead the procession. When I was a young man the eighteenth century was all round me, O'Leary and J. F. Taylor praised it and seemed of it, and I had been to a school where Pope was the only poet since Shakespeare and, because I wanted romantic furniture, ignored it.

Then later on, because every political opponent used it to cry down Irish literature that sought audience or theme in Ireland, I hated it. But now I am like that woman in Balzac who after a rich marriage and association with the rich, made in her old age the jokes of the concierge's lodge where she was born. I think constantly of some Irish lads I spoke to in California many years ago, and found as familiar with 'Young Ireland' as lads at home, because they gave me perhaps for the first time a sense of contact with a race scattered and yet one. My son who approaches his ninth year when told that Italy excelled in painting, England in poetry, Germany in music, asked in what Ireland excelled, and was told that Ireland must not be judged like other nations because it had only just won back its freedom. I may suggest to him, if I live long enough, that the thought of Swift, enlarged and enriched by Burke, saddled and bitted reality and that materialism was hamstrung by Berkeley, and ancient wisdom brought back; that modern Europe has known no men more powerful.

XII

I find this in Coleridge's *Fears in Solitude:*

"Meanwhile, at home,
All individual dignity and power
Engulfed in Courts, Committees, Institutions,
Associations and Societies."

I think of some saying of Mussolini's that power is the better for having a christian name and address. Balzac says that in France before the Revolution a man gathered friends about his table, formed a mimic court, but since it he satisfies ambition by founding a society and becoming its president or secretary. He seemed to see in such societies and the causes they fostered personal ambition. Compare the rule of the 'many' as described by Swift in his Greek and Roman essay. Balzac and Swift saw predatory instinct where Coleridge saw paralysis.

XIII

I find this in Coleridge's *Hexameters written during a temporary Blindness.* He is talking of the eye of a blind man:

"Even to him it exists, it stirs and moves in its
   prison;
Lives with a separate life, and 'Is it the Spirit' he
   murmurs:
Sure it has thoughts of its own and to see is only its
   language."

These lines written in 1799 "during temporary blindness", must be taken as the sense in which he understood Berkeley— that given by Charpentier. — Through the particular we approach the Divine Ideas— not I think the Berkeley of the *Commonplace Book*.

XIV

June 6th.
Why does Coleridge delight me more as man than poet? Even if I believed, and I do not, the general assumption that he established nothing of value, it would not affect the matter. I think the reason is that from 1807 or so he seems to have some kind of illumination which was, as always, only in part communicable. The end attained in such a life, is not a truth or even a symbol of truth, but a oneness with some spiritual being or beings. It is this that fixes our amazed attention on Oedipus when his death approaches, and upon some few historical men. It is because the modern philosopher has not sought this

that he remains unknown to those multitudes who thought his predecessors sacred. Perhaps Coleridge needed opium to recover a state which, some centuries earlier was accessible to the fixed attention of normal man.

June 13th.
No, that is not the explanation, for I have remembered that I thought with like pleasure of Mallarmé's talk to his famous circle. I think the explanation must explain also why, during the most creative years of my artistic life, when Synge was writing plays and Lady Gregory translated early Irish poetry with an impulse that interpreted my own, I disliked the isolation of the work of art. I wished through the drama, through a commingling of verse and dance, through singing that was also speech, through what I called the applied arts of literature to plunge it back into social life.

The use of dialect for the expression of the most subtle emotion — Synge's translation of Petrarch — verse where the syntax is that of common life, are but the complement of a philosophy spoken in the common idiom escaped from isolating method, gone back somehow from professor and pupil to Blind Tiresias.

XV

June 19th.
The other day I came home from a call upon a friend

very dissatisfied with my conversation. Presently I said to my wife: "Now that my vitality grows less I should set up as sage". She said: "What do you mean by that?" and I said "Adapt my conversation to the company instead of the company to my conversation". She said "It is too late to change". Now I have been running over those words of mine and wonder with sudden excitement if they do not account for emotion in the presence of things so unlike as Swift's epitaph, Berkeley in his *Commonplace Book* "We Irish do not think so", Burke at certain famous moments, Coleridge at Highgate, Mallarmé on his Thursday evenings. They, as did Blind Tiresias, talked to the occasion, and seeing that they did not scorn our drama, lips as living as those in Fragonard's "Fountain of Life" drink of their stream. In that grim and wise account of a Thebiad *The Lausiac History of Palladius*, men went on pilgrimage to St. Anthony that they might learn about their spiritual states, what was about to happen and why it happened, and St. Anthony would reply neither out of traditional casuistry nor commonsense but from supernatural power. When I think of Swift, of Burke, of Coleridge, of Mallarmé, I remember that they spoke as it were sword in hand, that they played their part in a unique drama, but played it, as a politician cannot though he stand in the same ranks, with the whole soul. Once or twice I have spoken words which came from nowhere, which I could not account for, which were even absurd, which have been fulfilled to the letter. I am trying to understand why certain metaphysicians whom I have spent years trying to master repel me, why those invisible beings I have learned to trust would turn me from all that is not conflict, that is not from sword in hand. Is it not like this? I cannot discover truth by logic unless that logic serve passion, and only then if the logic be ready to cut its own throat, tear out its own eyes— the cry of Hafiz "I made a bargain with that hair before the beginning of time", the cry of every lover. Those spiritual beings seem always as if they would turn me from every abstraction. I must not talk to myself about "the truth" nor call myself "teacher" nor another "pupil"— these things are abstract— but see myself set in a drama where I struggle to exalt and overcome concrete realities perceived not with mind only but as with the roots of my hair. The passionless reasoners are pariah dogs and devour the dead symbols. The clarified spirits own the truth, they have intellect; but we receive as agents, never as owners, in reward for victory.

XVI

Man can only love Unity of Being and that is why such conflicts are conflicts of the whole soul. Synge, for instance, must have felt compelled to his conflict with the pasteboard morality of political Dublin to make that world of his imagination more and more complete. If the man who sat behind me on the first night of *The Well of the Saints* and kept repeating "Blasphemy — blasphemy — more blasphemy —" had attended to the stage he would have discovered in the strange miracle worker, who comes and goes like cloud and rain, something, even, beyond the knowledge of its creator, a possibility of life not as yet in existence. All that our opponent expresses must be shown for a part of our greater expression, that he may become our thrall — be "enthralled" as they say. Yet our whole is not his whole and he may break away and enthrall us in his turn, and there arise between us a struggle like that of the sexes. All life is such a struggle. When a plant draws from and feeds upon the soil, expression is its joy, but it is wisdom to be drawn forth and eaten.

XVII

Even the most abstract thought has its conflict; Schoolman replies to Schoolman, but it is not of the whole nature. It is never as if we looked at the *Victory of Samothrace* and felt it in the soles of our feet.

XVIII

No matter how full the expression, the more it is of the whole man, the more does it require other expressions for its completion. As I watch *The Well of the Saints* upon the stage how can I help feeling that just as the actor's voice and forms enlarge the written words, there are actions or thoughts, could I but find them, that would complete it all.

Certain abstract thinkers, whose measurements and classifications contiually bring me back to concrete reality — the third book of *The World as Will and Idea*, Coleridge at Highgate. I think of the Tractarians, American transcendentalists at the first half of the nineteenth century and of the morbid profundity of French literature in its second half, though I do not know whether the influence of Schopenhauer or Flaubert and Beaudelaire was direct or but in the air. An abstract thinker when he has this relation to concrete reality passes on both the thought and the passion; who has not remains in the classroom.

XIX

Berkeley thought that by showing that certain abstractions — the 'primary qualities' — did not exist he could create a philosophy so concrete that the common people could understand it. Had he founded his university in Bermuda we would certainly have seen an attempt to make it so intelligible, though perhaps not a successful attempt, for the whole world was sinking into abstraction. Sometimes when I think of him, what flitted before his eyes flits before mine also, I half perceive a world like that of a Zen priest in Japan or in China, but am hurried back into abstraction after but an instant.

XX

During the year and a half in which Coleridge wrote almost all his good poetry, the first part of *Christabel*, *The Ancient Mariner*, *Kubla Khan*, he was influenced by Berkeley — the influence of Burke came later. Berkeley's insistence on the particular and his hatred of abstraction possibly delivered Coleridge from rhymed opinions, though but for a time. Face to face with the seeming contradiction between the early Berkeley and the Berkeley of *Siris* he calls sight "a language" . . . . . but if he means by this that through the particular we approach the Divine ideas, which was perhaps the thought of Berkeley's later life though not that of the *Commonplace Book* (In *Siris* 'light' must be 'sight'), this lacking some clear definition of those 'ideas' abstraction is once more upon us.

I can call them spaceless, timeless beings that behold and determine each other, but what can they be to monotheistic Burke and Coleridge but God's abstract or separate thoughts?

XXI

I think that two conceptions, that of reality as a congeries of beings, that of reality as a single being, alternate in our emotion and in history, and must always remain something that human reason, because subject always to one or the other, cannot reconcile. ⌊I am always, in all I do, driven to a moment which is the realisation of myself as unique and free, or to a moment which is the surrender to God of all that I am. I think that there are historical cycles wherein one or the other predominates, and that a cycle approaches where all shall (be) as particular and concrete as human intensity permits.⌋ Again and again I have tried to sing that approach, *The Hosting of the Sidhe*, "O sweet everlasting voices", and those lines about "The lonely, majestical multitude", and have almost understood my intention. ⌊Again and again with remorse, a sense of defeat, I have failed when I would write of God, written coldly and conventionally. Could those two impulses, one as much a part of truth as the other, be reconciled, or if one or the other could prevail, all life would cease.⌋

XXII

When I was in my twenties I saw a drawing or etching by some French artist of an angel standing against a midnight sky. The angel was old, wingless, and armed like a knight, as impossibly tall as one of those figures at Chartres Cathedral, and its face was worn by time and by innumerable battles.

I showed my father the drawing but he thought nothing of it because it was out of proportion, and I did not then know that an artist may exaggerate as he will for the sake of expression. Generally a judgment from my father would put me off anything, but this time that image remained and I imitated it in the old angels at the end of *The Countess Cathleen*. [I do not know whether it was before or after this that I made a certain girl see a vision of the Garden of Eden. She heard "the music of Paradise coming from the Tree of Life", and, when I told her to put her ear against the bark, that she might hear the better, found that it was made by the continuous clashing of swords.]

XXIII

[If men are born many times, as I think, that must originate in the antinomy between human and divine freedom. Man incarnating, translating "the divine ideas" into his language of the eye, to assert his own freedom, dying into the freedom of God and then coming to birth again. So too the assertions and surrender of sexual love, all that I have described elsewhere as antithetical and primary.] My father once said to me that contemplative men had been for centuries in conspiracy to exalt their form of life, and I think I remember his denying that painter and poet were contemplative. I think I assert this when

I assert that we hold down as it were on the sword's point what would, if undefeated, grow into the counter-truth, that when our whole being lives we create alike out of our love and hate.

XXIV

Plotinus calls well-nigh the most beautiful of Enneads* *The Impassivity of the Disembodied* but, as he was compelled to at his epoch, thought of man as re-absorbed into God's freedom as final reality. The ultimate reality must be all movement, all thought, all perception extinguished, two freedoms unthinkably, unimaginably absorbed in one another. Surely if either circuit, that which carries us into man or that which carries us into God, were reality, the generation had long since found its term.

XXV

The other day Gogarty wrote that John wanted to do a "serious portrait". I replied that "I would think it a great honour". And today I have been standing in front of the hotel mirror noticing certain lines about my mouth and chin marked strongly by shadows cast from a window on my right, and have wondered if John would not select those very lines and lay great emphasis upon them, and, if some friend complain that he has obliterated what good

---

*The Third Ennead "The Impassivity of the Unembodied" translated by Stephen MacKenna.

looks I have, insist that those lines show character, and perhaps that there are no good looks but character. In those lines I see the marks of recent illness, marks of time, growing irresolution, perhaps some faults that I have long dreaded; but then my character is so little myself that all my life it has thwarted me. It has affected my poems, my true self, no more than the character of a dancer affects the movement of the dance. When I was painted by John years ago, and saw for the first time the portrait (or rather the etching taken from it) now in a Birmingham gallery, I shuddered.

Always particular about my clothes, never dissipated, never unshaved except during illness, I saw myself there an unshaven, drunken bar-tender, and then I began to feel John had found something that he liked in me, something closer than character, and by that very transformation made it visible. He had found Anglo-Irish solitude, a solitude I have made for myself, an outlawed solitude.

XXVI

June 23rd.

Have we exhausted Deism, even that form which Blake denounced as pagan nature worship, which Wordsworth got from Coleridge? Certainly none of the writers who are most characteristic of our time turn it into poetry. Neither James Joyce, who is, someone tells me, a Thomist, nor T. S. Eliot who is certainly Anglican. In so far as we believe that reality is a congeries we shall be uncertain of victory. We and those other souls to whom we are as it were bound and sworn, with whom we share a morality, may be defeated, and to those who believe in the final victory of Good there is greater heroism in our uncertainty. In morality itself there may be something arbitrary, as in the morals of Oedipus, as perhaps in all morality before the philosophy of Unity prevailed, as if it were the special discipline of a class, or a city, or a regiment. A young man* who was killed after he had been twice decorated, said to me, "I joined up out of friendship". Yet there is always the other truth: "Thou, Thou alone art everlasting, and the blessed spirits whom Thou includest as the sea its waves".

XXVII

Spiritualism seems to announce such changes by its immense vogue; all that has to do with Christ, or angels, or Deism, — unlike the Swedenborgians who gave it doctrinal form — is sentimental make-belief, a pantomime stage where disembodied spirits re-create their human loves and hates.

XXVIII

If reality is timeless and spaceless this is a goal, an

* Robert Gregory.

ultimate Good. But if I believe that is also a congeries of autonomous selves I cannot believe in one ever victorious providence, though I may in providences that preside over a man, a class, a city, a nation, a world — providences that may be defeated, the Tutelary spirits of Plotinus.

XXIX

Two men of great ability, one rather famous, have said to me this winter, in repudiation of what they believed my thought, that the ultimate reality must be anarchy. I remember madame Blavatsky, when alone with me and one other, talking of "God-chaos, the which every man is seeking in his heart". By the study of those impulses that shape themselves into words without context we find our thought, for we do not seek truth in argument or in books but clarification of what we already believe. It is for this reason that we hate those confident men and books who as it were trample in their top-boots or crack their whips between our cradles. Dissatisfaction with the old idea of God cannot but overthrow our sense of order for the new conception of reality has not even begun to develop, it is still a phantom not a child.

XXX

Renvyle. July 23rd.
I have talked most of a long motor journey, talked

even when I was hoarse. Why? Surely because I was timid, because I felt the other man was judging me, because I endowed his silence with all kinds of formidable qualities. Being on trial I must cajole my judge.

XXXI

We approach influx. What is its form? A civilisation lasts two thousand years from nadir to nadir — Christ came at the Graeco-Roman meridian, physical maturity spirit in celestial body, and was the first beginning of the One — all equal in the eyes of One. Our civilisation which began in A.D. 1,000 approaches the meridian and once there must see the counter-birth. What social form will that birth take? It is multitudinous, the seal of the congeries of autonomous beings each seeing all within its own unity. I can only conceive of it as society founded upon unequal rights and unequal duties which if fully achieved would include all nations in the European stream in one harmony, where each drew its nourishment from all though each drew different nourishment. But this ideal will be no more achieved than are the equal rights and duties before the One — God with the first Christians, Reason with Rousseau. There will be a weak unforseen life moulding itself upon poor thought, war in all likelihood, discord till it become in its turn concord (spirit in celestial body)

Olympus just as it breaks. It is founded by a Teacher not a Victim, and this Teacher is what he is because he creates and expresses the congeries, or concord of many, which must impose itself in the course of centuries. No, as Daimon of a desperation he is that congeries, the family, the race, any group which is a kindred of any kind as distinct from an organised opinion. He will be preceded by opinion, but the influx can only be kindred— the two daimons, the four daimons. He is not a being but a harmony of beings.]

Spengler is right when he says all who preserve tradition will find their opportunity. Tradition is kindred. The abrogation of equality of rights and duties is because duties should depend on rights, rights on duties. If I till and dig my land I should have rights because of that duty done, and if I have much land that, according to all ancient races, should bring me still more rights. But if I have much or little land and neglect it I should have few rights. This is the theory of Fascism and so far as land is concerned it has the history of the earth to guide it and that is permanent history. A day will come however, when man's ever increasing plasticity will make possible and compel a decision among the rights and duties which constitute refined society. Shall we grant the nun and the lady of fashion their leisure? Can we call their refinement duty and therefore the leisure essential to it a right? If so, what kind of lady, what kind of nun? We can no longer point to history for we are plastic, as Flinders Petrie might say we are no longer archaic, we control our material. The answer will not be given by man.

Can such a kindred once formed escape war? Will it not be war that must prove its strength? Its dead will return to it after death for there can be no other fitting environment, and if it has religious ceremonies those ceremonies will remember this. I think of the Mormons, their baptisms for the dead, the ceremonies that offer their wisdom to the dead. Yet I must bear in mind that an antithetical revelation will be less miraculous (in the sense of signs and wonders) more psychological than a primary which is from beyond man and mothered by the void. It is developed out of man and is man.

XXXII

Landed property gets its fascination from its inequality: divide it up into farms of equal size or fertility and it would still retain its inequality, no field or hedge like another.

When I was a young man I hated the solitary book, abstraction because its adepts sat in corners to pull out their solitary plums. The sight of Yvette Guilbert, a solitary, a performer to an alien crowd, filled me with distaste, for I would have seen her in some great house among her equals and her friends. I wanted a theatre where the greatest passions and all the permanent interests of men might be displayed that we might find them not alone over a book but, as I said again and again, lover by lover, friend by friend. All I wanted was impossible, and I wore out my youth in its pursuit, but now I know it is the mystery to come.

August 9th. Coole Park.
Swift's . . . .* is more important to modern thought than Vico and certainly foreshadowed Flinders Petrie, Frobenius, Henry Adams, Spengler, and very exactly and closely Gerald Heard. It needs interpretation, for it had to take the form of a pamphlet intelligible to the Whig nobility. He saw civilisations 'exploding' — to use Heard's term, just before the final state, and that final state as a tyranny, and he took from a Latin writer the conviction that every civilisation carries with it from the first what shall bring it to an end. Burke borrowed of him or re-discovered and Coleridge borrowed from Burke all but that inevitable end. Without the passion and style of either, Coleridge found through his very langour and hesitation time to approve the motives

* A Discourse of the Contests and Dissensions between the Nobles and the Commons in Athens and Rome.

of acts that he hated. "The victory of the Plebs" was "explosive" but it originated in our civilisation from the misapplication of "pure thought" which rightly applied is religion or philosophy. Though Luther was right to grant free judgment Rousseau was not right, for though we have all the "reason" "pure thought" or conscience that judges motives, we have not all "the understanding" or prudence to judge of acts and their consequences. There are children, even the French Revolution did not give them votes, lunatics, drunkards, dullards, persons too busy for thought or too dependent upon others to express it. All have "reason" but not all have "the means of exercising it and the materials the facts and ideas upon which it is exercised" nor have all that have the means "power of attention". Historical society is founded upon these difficulties but when we ignore them we create a government only possible among those that need no government. Swift thought that we set free a multitude of private interests to overbear all who by privilege of station, genius or training possessed the puplic mind, and thereby at last created a situation that had no issue but despotism. Roman history, as he saw it, was a struggle of classes but Greek history, where the governing class was broken before history began, was the driving out or putting to death of all illustrious soldiers and statesmen. I think of Swift's own life, of the letter where he describes his love of this man and of that, and his hatred of all classes and professions. I remember his epitaph and understand that the liberty he served was that of intellect, not liberty for the masses but for those who could make it visible.

When Gulliver on the magical island is bid call up what ghosts he will, he calls up seven, all but one — Sir Thomas More — from Greece or Rome, seven exiled or murdered men to whom the world cannot add an eighth. Certainly when Swift describes the Houyhnhnms as "the perfection of nature", he meant, like Rousseau, simplicity, but Swift's simplicity, was the achievement of solitary men. Coleridge describes how social philosophers foretold that the French Revolution would be followed by despotism and were mocked at in the press because though such had happened from like cause in the past it could not happen in the "enlightened eighteenth century"; but when he would show the cause in action he lacks the lucidity of Berkeley and Swift. His description of France, all historical inequalities swept away, as a machine ready for Napoleon, reminds me that Kropotkin upon the one occasion when we talked — though I had often seen him — said that the Revolution by sweeping away old communal customs and institutions in the name of equal rights and duties left the French peasant at the mercy of the capitalist.

What has set me writing is Coleridge's proof, which seems to me conclusive, that civilisation is driven to its final phase not by the jealousy and egotism of the many, as Swift's too simple statement implies, but by "pure thought" "reason", what my System calls "spirit" and "celestial body", by that which makes all places and persons alike; that clay comes before the potter's thumb. I remember that my 'instructors' instance that understanding the "faculties" wears thin at the end of an age, and begin to speculate about the plasticity that is the theme of Mr. Wyndham Lewis in *The Apes of God* and of Pirandello at all time.

Has "pure thought" changed its ground, and so dissolved those historical forms and occupations wherefrom we have drawn our personalities, that we must take every chance suggestion, or deliberately create a personality and live henceforth as Homunculus in his bottle? Flinders Petrie shows where in the history of a civilisation sculpture, painting, mechanism, will put off what he calls archaism and gain control of their material, and, because vigour implies effort, begin their decline. Are those amusing people described by Mr. Wyndham Lewis not the first of a great multitude who put in control and invited to create without a model must make ready for the tyrant.

At the end of an epoch or civilisation I imagine a maturity, not of this or that science or art or condition, but, in so far as may be possible considering time and place, of the civilisation itself an instant before its dissolution or transformation when it may, wherever it is most sensitive, submit not to this or that external tyrant but to a Being or an Olympus all can share.

August 10th.

"Pure thought" because it is concedes all universals finds all alike, leaves all plastic, and its decisions, did it dwell equally in all men, would be a simultaneous decision, a world-wide general election, a last judgment, and for judge a terrible Christ like that in the Apse at Cefalu.*

But the understanding because founded upon experience, upon many lives, let us say, cannot submit its decision or the vote of a moment, once more the antimony.

Did Swift deliberately set "pure thought" aside? He advised his clergy to preach the mysteries of religion once or twice a year and then speak no more of what none can or should understand. He thought missionaries in China should say nothing about Christ's

* Monreale Cathedral, Sicily.

divinity and said that the first Christians thought it "too high" for general understanding and so kept silent about it. He prayed much, had the Communion Service by heart, but he received dogma and ritual from the State and condemned Huguenot and Dissenter alike. He was at one time the friend, the benefactor perhaps, of Berkeley, but never speaks of his philosophy.

September 9th.

Berkeley's essay on *Passive Obedience* asks a question that Berkeley, through the lack of the historical sense, cannot answer. Dreading, as Swift dreaded, a return of public disorder he forbids opposition to the State under all circumstances, though when such opposition has arisen, and the headship of the State is vacant or in doubt a (man) may choose his party. No modern man can accept a conclusion that confounds red and white armies alike. Burke answered the question, and Swift, had he taken up again the thought of his essay on the *Dissensions of the Greeks and Romans*, could have answered it. Berkeley spoke his speech in the great drama of Anglo-Irish thought. The answer came when the curtain rose upon the second act. A state is organic and has its childhood and maturity and, as Swift saw and Burke did not, its decline. We owe allegiance to the government of our day in so far as it embodies that historical being.

September 11th.

Last night a dream which I dream several times a year — a great house which I recognise as partly Coole and partly Sandymount Castle — though not by any exact physical resemblance. In all these dreams Sandymount gives the tragic element — in one which I remember vividly the house was built round a ruin and Sandymount was the ruin. This time all the house was castellated and about to pass into other hands, its pictures auctioned. I remember looking at a picture and thinking that it would now lose its value, for its value was that it had always hung in a particular place and had been put there by some past member of the family. Coole as a Gregory house is near its end, it will be before long an office and residence for foresters, a little cheap furniture in the great rooms a few religious oleographs its only pictures, and yet when in my dream I had some such thought I stood in a Gothic door which I now recognise as the door at Sandymount. I never think of Sandymount Castle and would not have seen it except from the road had I not been shown over it by the headmaster of the school that had what remained, the garden disappeared long ago. The impression on my subconscious was made in childhood, when my uncle Corbet's death and bankruptcy was a recent tragedy, the book with Sandymount Castle printed on the cover open upon my knees. I vividly recall those photographs of ornamental waters, of a little rustic bridge, of the oak room where celebrated men had sat down to breakfast, of garden paths, of a great door suggesting not Abbotsford but Strawberry Hill — the door that my dream recalled.

Yet do I speak the truth when I say I never think of it? The other day at my uncle Isaac's funeral I thought how little I had seen of him and that fear had kept me away. He was so much better bred than I — he had about him the sweetness of those gardens, so too have my old aunts who spent their childhood there. I have intellect, scornful, impatient, dissatisfied and always a little ashamed.

September 12th.

⌈Berkeley in the *Commonplace Book* thought that "we perceive" and are passive whereas God creates in perceiving. He creates what we perceive. I substitute for God the Thirteenth Cone, the Thirteenth Cone therefore creates our perceptions — all the visible world — as held in common by our wheel.⌋

The chair in which I am sitting is covered in black silk with a pattern of pale pink roses with pale green leaves. This silk is from the dress worn by Lady Gregory when presented at Court. I think of my Japanese sword wrapped in a piece of silk from a Japanese lady's Court dress.

XXXIII
A letter to Michael's Schoolmaster.

Dear Sir

My son is now between nine and ten and should begin Greek at once and be taught by the Berlitz method that he may read as soon as possible that most exciting of all stories, the Odyssey, from that landing in Ithica to the end. Grammar should come when the need comes. As he grows older he will read to me the great lyric poets and I will talk to him about Plato. Do not teach him one word of Latin. The Roman people were the classic decadence, their literature form without matter. They destroyed Milton, the French seventeenth and our own eighteenth century, and our schoolmasters even today read Greek with Latin eyes. Greece, could we but approach it with eyes as young as its own, might renew our youth. Teach him mathematics as thoroughly as his capacity permits. I know that Bertrand Russell must, seeing that he is such a featherhead, be wrong about everything but as I have no mathematics I cannot prove it. I do not want my son to be as helpless. Do not teach him one word of geography. He has lived on the Alps, crossed a number of rivers and when he is fifteen I shall urge him to climb the Sugar Loaf. Do not teach him a word of history. I shall take him to Shakespeare's history plays, if a commercialised theatre permit, and give him all the historical novels of Dumas, and if he cannot pick up the rest he is a fool. Dont teach him one word of science, he can get all he wants in the newspapers and in any case it is no job for a gentleman. If you teach him Greek and mathematics and do not let him forget the French and German that he already knows you will do for him all that one man can do for another. If he wants to learn Irish after he is well founded in Greek, let him — it will clear his eyes of the Latin miasma. If you will not do what I say, whether the curriculum or your own will restrain, and my son comes from school a smatterer like his father may your soul lie chained on the Red Sea bottom.

XXXIV

September 13th.

I met at Miss Grigsby's two months ago a New York clairvoyant — a woman — I forget her name or never knew it. Knew I had been ill: said "You are through with illness, should have ten wonderful years. It is unfortunate that spiritual change is impossible without illness." Spoke of my philosophic work, saw it do something I would hate — found "a cult". She spoke of notes written for my own eye and said that their publication would be very successful, seemed to think more of them than of the more serious work. Before I finished them I would however do something quite simple at the suggestion of a woman, "about a beggar, no, not exactly a beggar". Is this my Swift play? My wife who urged me to do it added the detail about the medium refusing money and then looking to see what each gave.]

XXXV

September 15th.

Reading Hone's unpublished life of Berkeley* I get that sense of unreality before the historical figure that I had before the portrait in the Fellows' Room in T.C.D.*² That philanthropic serene Bishop, that pasteboard man, never wrote the *Commonplace Book*. Attracted beyond expression by Berkeley's thought I have been repelled by the man as we have received him from tradition. A saint and sage who takes to tar water, who turns from the most overwhelming philosophic generalisations since Plato to convert negroes, and who in *Siris* writes as if he had forgotten it. But now that I reject the saint and sage I find Berkeley lovable. The Berkeley of the *Commonplace Book* wore an alien mask, the mask of preposterous benevolence that prevailed in sculpture and painting down to the middle of the nineteenth century— the monument to the Prince-Consort on Leinster Lawn

---

*Bishop Berkeley, by J. M. Hone and M. M. Rossi, with an introduction by W. B. Yeats. 1931.

*²Trinity College, Dublin.

— to hide his clamorous, childlike, naive, mischievous curiosity. The mischief of a man is malicious when he puts the skeleton out of the cupboard he calculates the whole effect, but Berkeley knew nothing of men and women. He loved discourse for its own sake as a child does, and said out of the contented solitude of a child the most embarrassing things. What did he really say in those three sermons to undergraduates that got him into such a political mess— not quite I think what he says in that irrational essay on *Passive Obedience* written to save his face. Was the Bermuda project more than a justification for curiosity and discourse? Was not that curiosity already half satisfied when he drew the plans of his learned city— a steeple in the centre and markets in the corners?

He left behind those three earnest Fellows of College who might have liked converting negroes— even today there is a T.C.D. mission to savage parts— and brought to America a portrait painter and a couple of pleasant young men of fortune, and when he got there associated with fox-hunters and American "Immaterialist" disciples. When Walpole refused the money he came home without apparent regret— and as I think, with relief. His curiosity was satisfied. Had an American disciple turned Boswell and had the genius for the task, we would have had another *Commonplace Book*, the old theme with vivid new illustrations drawn from the passing show. He returned to Ireland, the eighteenth century mask—itself one of those abstractions he denounced—clapped firmly on his face. There is a famine in Ireland; a Bishop must be benevolent, besides a child has never thought of being anything else, but his curiosity is even more powerful. Had he not been told in America of Indians that cured all kinds of things with a concoction of tar? He had already put the mathematicians and philosophers by the ears, why not the doctors? And the tar water, and the cures it worked, what a subject for discourse! Could he not lead his reader—especially if that reader drank tar water every morning—from tar to light? Newton, made ignorant by his very knowledge, his contact with other men, his lack of childish solitude, had postulated an Ether, an abstraction, a something that did not exist because unperceived. If this is a foundation stuff it has visibility, light—mind and light the Siamese twins that constitute the whole of reality. But he is also the burned child so he writes as if he had never heard of Immaterialism, he becomes a materialist stoic philosopher, playing with some harmless symbol. The American Samuel Johnson and his Irish disciples will understand that this light, this intellectual Fire, is that continuity which holds together "the perceptions", that it is a substitute for the old symbol God. Is it to adjust his mask more carefully, to pose himself as it were against remote antiquity, or a need for symbol that makes him talk of the Neoplatonic Trinity?

When I think of him, I think of my father, and of others born into the Anglo-Irish solitude, of their curiosity, their discourse, their spontaneity, their irresponsibility, their innocence, their sense of mystery as they grow old, their readiness to dress up at the suggestion of others though never quite certain what dress they wear.

Berkeley the Bishop was a humbug. His wife, that charming daughter who played the viol, Queen Caroline, Ministers of State, imposed it upon him; but he was meant for a Greek tub or an Indian palm tree. Only once in his life was he free, when, still an undergraduate, he filled *The Commonplace Book* with snorts of defiance.

Descartes, Locke and Newton took away the world and give us its excrement instead. Berkeley restored the world. I think of the Nirvana Song of the Japanese Monk: "I sit on the mountain side and look up at the little farm— I say to the old farmer: 'How many times have you mortgaged your land and paid off the mortgagee?.' I take pleasure in the sound of the reeds".

Berkeley has brought back to us the world that only exists because it shines and sounds. A child, smothering its laughter because the elders are standing round, has opened once more the great box of toys.

XXXVI

September 20th.

Toyohiko Kagawa like Gandhi seems to rely on a subtlety of moral understanding no popular leader can rely upon in Europe. It is the Divine Man as an organising force. America and Russia have founded labour politics or "mutual aid", but how can there be mutual aid between "a labour group" and the sick, the old, "the foundling picked up at the street corner" or any other person "who cannot earn a living"? We should give without seeking a return. He interprets Genesis as the creation of the human soul. God created Eden for the unborn souls of Adam and Eve. A love for others must in the same way include their lives, their lives which are as yet unknown and unlived. We re-make the world for the sake of those lives. Karl Marx puts too much emphasis upon this re-made world and not enough upon the living; only when we contemplate those living can we re-make the world. The re-creation is from love of the perfect and mercy for the imperfect. He insists that love is always creative— "The husband expresses himself to his wife". "Love is creation raised to a higher degree". He talks much of love in connection with evolution. "In desire there is no selection — selection is love". This love when it forgives is God's love for then mercy is added. "When God's creative power, which formed heaven and earth, comes into me there is born in my heart the love that forgives the sinner".

He says "There lies buried in the Cosmos a love which does not rise to the level of human consciousness but is like the root buried underneath the stem". It elaborated the placenta of the higher animals. He thinks that the command "Love your enemies" may come from this root.

He quotes a certain Kuriyagawa Hakuson as saying "A love surpassing sexual desire comes into being — it may be called passionate love", is mutual and in all its forms creates physical love. Passionate love is a form of psychic love; psychic love forms a group of two or more, it selects those who are akin to us. It does not tolerate any who are outside the kindred, the kindred or group persecutes all those who are too slow or too fast. The final love is conscientious love. A single sinner makes all the Universe suffer — it suffers as we do from a wound in a finger and as all our blood might flow out in the small wound so might the life of the Universe flow out. This suffering is the suffering of God which we share in "conscientious love". "The sufferings of every individual become the defects and agonies of the whole world". "If we wish to live complete human lives we must atone for the sins of others. God to perfect his own life upon the earth saves beings who are imperfect".

The fish in "the miracle of the fishes" finding themselves excluded from the Kindred may have called Christ's love "psychic". A Japan which had completely accepted the christianity of Kagawa might be attacked; it would still need oil, metals, tillage and pasture, still have hungry neighbours, still need soldiers and their psychic love, be still caught in the whirl. Yet how shall we arouse the multitude if we admit that our truths are partial?

He speaks of the love the Sumari gave to his Lord in "return for his ration of rice" as "physical love". But this is to confuse the love with its occasion. It may have come from a deeper consciousness than that of those poverty-stricken Findlanders he praises because they sent money to the sufferers from the earthquake in Tokio. When we come to balance the two forms of noble feeling one against the other we feel most confident in that given to a known living man.

I write this paragraph to protect myself against the fascination of Toyohiko Kagawa and his heroic life.

XXXVII

September 26th.
In the Times Supplement for September 18th. 1930 a reviewer, apparently writing from personal knowledge, says: "Mr. Sassoon was relied upon especially for actions of a markedly dangerous sort (no doubt he was summed up as a 'fire eater')" I have read in some newspaper a letter from a private soldier speaking of the men's admiration and trust and a statement that when ordered to more comfortable and safe work in Egypt he petitioned the authorities to be sent back to France.

> "Do thou not grieve nor blush to be,
> As all th' inspired and tuneful men,
> And all thy great forefathers were
> From Homer down to Ben."
>   Cowley from the Essay "Myself".

XXXVIII

Kagawa thus describes future parliaments: "Parliaments of the present represent blind lotteries. In the new genuine society the representatives of the people will not be elected in this ridiculous fashion. All groups bound together industrially or psychically will as a rule have their representatives fixed; the representatives will express the will of their groups and make laws by mutual concession and inter-dependence and they will be free from hatred and slander". "Those who govern will be experts in social science, and the law-making bodies will be councils possessing affinities of conscience and representing all the elements which compose society".

XXXIX

When I was a young man I used to discuss mystical experience with Kabbalists in a little restaurant near the British Museum long passed away; we spoke of nothing more often than of those "pictures in the astral light" which had been until very lately "a secret of the mystical societies". Some man, whose name I forget, insisted that the mind in such a picture when it came into relation with our own could still create, though always within the limits of the picture. In such discussions the speaker would often describe some experience, and today I constantly find myself confirming with some philosophic argument what that man learned from tradition and experience. I too have had such experience and others "spiritualistic" in type which I shall publish when ready— to adapt a metaphor from Erasmus — to make myself a post for dogs and journalists to defile. The pictures seem of two kinds. There are those described in the last verse of *The Sensitive Plant*

"For love, and beauty, and delight
There is no death nor change; their might
Exceeds our organs, which endure
No light, being themselves obscure."

To the second kind belongs that of the shade of Achilles in the Odyssey drawing its bow as though still in the passion of battle, while the true spirit of Achilles is on Olympus with his wife Hebe. To it belong also those apparitions of the murderer still dragging his victim, of the miser still counting his money, of the suicide still hanging from his rafter.

We become aware of those of the first kind when some symbol, shaped by the experience itself, has descended to us, and when we ourselves have passed, through a shifting of the threshold consciousness, into a similar state.

The second kind, because it has no universal virtue, because it is altogether particular, is related only to the soul whose creation it is, though we can sometimes perceive it through association of place or of some object. It was the opinion of those Kabbalist friends that the actions of life remained so pictured but that the intensity of the light depended upon the intensity of the passion that had gone to their creation. This is to assume, perhaps correctly, that the greater the passion the more clear the perception, for the light is perception. "Light" said Grossetete "is corporeality itself or that of which corporeality is made", whereas Bonaventura calls taste and smell forms of light. The "pictures" appear to be self-luminous because the past sunlight or candle light, suddenly made apparent, is as it were broken off from whatever light surrounds it at the moment. Passion is conflict, consciousness is conflict.

Blake did not use the words "picture" but spoke of the bright sculptures of Los's Halls from which all love stories renew themselves, and that remain on, that one does not see the picture as it appeared to the living actor but the action itself, and that we feel as if we could walk round it as if there was no fixed point of view. Whose perception then do we share? I put this point once to my instructors. They replied that the "picture" had nothing to do with memory — it was not a remembered perception — and left me to find the explanation. I have to face Berkeley's greatest difficulty: to account for the continuity of perception, but my problem is limited to the continuity of the perception that constitutes, in my own and other eyes, my body and its acts. That continuity is in the Passionate Body of the permanent self or daimon. Should I see the ghost of murderer and victim I should do so because my Spirit has from those other Passionate Bodies fabricated light, or perception. That fabrication is not enforced by the Passionate Body, is an act of attention on my Spirit's part; but for the act the presence of the murderer's own Spirit must be present, for as the Passionate Body is not in space and can only be found through its Spirit or daimon which is only present during its moments of retrocession or sleep I should have said not that the living mind of Keats or Shakespeare but their daimon is present and the Passionate Bodies that constituted its moment, for images in the mind acquire their identity also from the Passionate Body. The daimon of Shakespeare or a Keats has however entered into a sleepless universality.

October 17th.
Light then — colour, light and shade — fabricated by the intellect and changed with its forms is perception, that which gives a visible unity to the multiple Passionate Body.

The "perception", may be considered as a circle or space of light encircling each man, and it is the Husk. The dead past thrown off by the living present.

XL

Three Essentials.
I would found literature on the three things which Kant thought we must postulate to make life livable. — Freedom, God, Immortality. The fading of these three before "Bacon, Newton, Locke" has made

literature decadent. Because Freedom is gone we have Stendhal's "mirror dawdling down a lane;" because God has gone we have realism, the accidental, because Immortality is gone we can no longer write those tragedies which have always seemed to me alone legitimate— those that are a joy to the man who dies. Recent Irish literature has only delighted me in so far as it implies one or the other, in so far as it has been a defiance of all else, in so far as it has created those extravagant characters and emotions which have always arisen spontaneously from the human mind when it sees itself exempt from death and decay, responsible to its source alone.

James Joyce differs from Arnold Bennett and Galsworthy, let us say, because he can isolate the human mind and its vices as if in eternity. So could Synge, so could O'Casey till he caught the London contagion in *The Silver Tassie* and changed his mountain into a mouse. The movement began with A.E's first little verses made out of the *Upanishads*, and my *Celtic Twilight* a bit of ornamental trivial needlework sown on a prophetic fury got by Blake and Boehme. James Stephens has read the *Tain* in the light of the *Veda* but the time is against him and he is silent.

Between Berkeley's account of his exploration of certain Kilkenny laws which speak of the "natives" came that intellectual crisis which led up to the sentence in *The Commonplace Book* "We Irish do not think so". That was the birth of the national intellect and it aroused the defeat in Berkeley's philosophical secret society of English materialism, the Irish Salamis.

The capture of a Spanish treasure ship in the time of Elizabeth made England a capitalist nation, a nation of country gentlemen, who were paid more in kind than in money and had traditional uses for their money, were to find themselves in control of free power over labour, a power that could be used anywhere and for anything.

The first nation that can affirm the three convictions affirmed by Kant as free powers — i.e. without associations of language, dogma and ritual — will be able to control the moral energies of the soul.
October 19th.
It is I think because those convictions must return as free power that I feel, that so many feel, an unreality in French neo-Thomist movements, in T. S. Eliot's revival of seventeenth century divines.
In the time of Swift, of Burke and of Coleridge the habitual symbols seemed necessary to the order; Swift, who almost certainly hated sex, looked upon

himself, he says somewhere, as appointed to guard a position; and tradition could claim the still unquestioned authority of the Bible. But today the man who finds belief in God, in the soul, in immortality, growing and clarifying, is blasphemous and paradoxical. He must above all things free his energies from all prepossessions not imposed by those beliefs themselves. The Fascist, the Bolshevist, seeks to turn the idea of the State into free power and both have reached (though the idea of the State as it is in the mind of the Bolshevist is dry and lean) some shadow of that intense energy which shall come to those of whom I speak.

When I speak of the three convictions and of the idea of the State I do not mean any metaphysical or economic theory. That belief which I call free power is free because we cannot distinguish between the things believed in and the belief; it is something forced upon us bit by bit; as it liberates our energies we sink in on truth.

An idea of the State which is not a preparation for those three convictions, a State founded on economics alone, would be a prison house. A State must be made like a Chartres Cathedral for the glory of God and the soul. It exists for the sake of the virtues and must pay their price. The uneconomic leisure of scholars, monks and women gave us truth, sanctity and manners. Free power is not the denial of that past but such a conflagration or integration of that past that it can be grasped in a single thought.

Now that we think of the Gospels as evidence, not of an historical event, but of the mind of the early church, we discover that mind not so much like our own as like what it will be when the clock has run down when the dissolution of tradition is complete. I notice already men who suggest the Greek in his tub, the Fakir under his tree. I even connect with that coming State our emotion at the thought of crowds that seem beloved history, Synge's work, James Stephens' strange exciting figures. Is not the Bolshevist's passion for the machine, his creation in the theatre and the schools of mass emotion, a parody of what we feel. We are casting off crown and mitre that we may lay our heads on mother earth.

But I am no believer in Milleniums. I but forsee another moment of plasticity and disquiet like that which was at and before the commencement of our era, re-shaped by the moral impulse preserved in the Gospels, and that other present, according to Mr. Mackail, in Virgil. At the moment more important that I should try the lots in Virgil than in the Gospels. What idea of the State, what substitute for that of the Toga'd race that rules the world, will serve our immediate purpose here in Ireland?

History is necessity until it takes fire in some one's head and becomes freedom or virtue. Berkeley's Salamis was such a conflagration, another is about us now?

When I try to make a practical rule I come once more to a truism — serve nothing from the heart that is not its own evidence, what Blake called "naked beauty displayed" recognise that the rest is machinery and should (be) used as such. The great men of the eighteenth century were that beauty; Parnell had something of it, O'Leary something, but what has O'Connell and all his seed, breed and generation but a roaring machine? Is the Gaelic revival, if the school books are full, as a saintly old nun said to me, of pot-house literature anything but a machine? Let us become homeless, helpless, obscure, that we may live by handiwork alone. One day thirty years ago, walking with Douglas Hyde I heard haymakers sing what he recognised as his own words and I begged him to give up all coarse oratory that he might sing such words. The factories will never run short of hands, and yet

> We built Nineveh with our sighs,
> And Babel itself with our mirth.

Preserve that which is living and help the two Irelands, Gaelic Ireland and Anglo Ireland so to unite that neither shall shed its pride. Study the great problems of the world, as they have been lived in our scenery, the re-birth of European spirituality in the mind of Berkeley, the restoration of European order in the mind of Burke. Every nation is the whole world in a mirror and our mirror has twice been very bright and clear. Do not be afraid to boast so long as the boast lays burdens on the boaster. Study the educational system of Italy, the creation of the philosopher Gentile, where even religion is studied not in the abstract but in the minds and lives of Italian saints and thinkers, it becomes at once part of Italian history.

As for the rest we wait till the world changes and its reflection changes in our mirror and an hieratical society returns, power descending from the few to the many, from the subtle to the gross, not because some man's policy has decreed it but because what is so overwhelming cannot be restrained. A new beginning, a new turn of the wheel.
October 20th.
We have not an Irish Nation until all classes grant its right to take life according to the law and until it is certain that the threat of invasion made by no matter who would rouse all classes to arms. When Grattan's volunteers were formed such an Ireland

seemed all but born. The refusal or postponement of Catholic Emancipation by the Irish Parliament brought disorder and the Act of Union. We have something like the same situation today with the actors reversed. One of the actors however has changed his habits. Anglo Ireland attends Church but has no dogmas, even less theology is read in Ireland than in other Protestant countries. There is hardly one of all those who sing hymns and say prayers perhaps even twice upon a Sunday who could see the absurdity of the theology in *Blanco Posnet* or think that it mattered if he did. This Anglo Ireland which accepts many Catholics has accepted the Free State after much hesitation. It would not spring to arms in its defence. Will the devout Catholicism and enthusiastic Gaeldom commit the error committed at the close of the eighteenth century by dogmatic Protestantism? Much of the emotional energy in our civil war came from the indignant denial of the right of the State, as at present established, to take life in its own defence, whether by arms or by process of law, and that right is still denounced by a powerful minority. Only when all permit the State to demand the voluntary or involuntary sacrifice of its citizens' lives will Ireland possess that moral unity to which England, according to Coleridge, owes so large a part of its greatness. All

I can see clearly, bound as I am within my own limited art, is that our moral unity is brought nearer by every play, poem or novel that is characteristically Irish.

XLI

When the directors of the Abbey Theatre rejected *The Silver Tassie* they did so because they thought it a bad play and a play which would mar the fame and popularity of its writer. It would seem from its failure in London that we were right, upon the other hand Mr. Shaw's and Mr. Augustus John's admiration suggest that it was at least better than we thought it, and yet I am certain that if any of our other dramatists sent us a similar play we would reject it. We were biased, we are biased, by the Irish Salamis. The war, as O'Casey has conceived it, is an equivalent for those primary qualities brought down by Berkeley's secret society, it stands outside the characters, it is not part of their expression, it is that very attempt denounced by Mallarmé to build as if with brick and mortar within the pages of a book. The English critics feel differently, to them a theme that "bulks largely in the news" gives dignity to human nature, even raises it to international importance. We on the other hand are certain that nothing can give dignity to human nature but the character and energy of its expression. We do not

even ask that it shall have dignity so long as it can burn away all that is not itself.
November 18th.
Science, separated from philosophy, is the opium of the suburbs.

Here ends "Pages from a Diary written in 1930" by W. B. Yeats. Two hundred and eighty copies of this book, of which two hundred and fifty are for sale, have been set in Caslon type, and printed by Esther Ryan and Maire Gill on paper made in Ireland, and published by The Cuala Press, 46 Palmerston Road, Dublin, Ireland. Finished in the second week of September nineteen hundred and forty four.

This is number

Reprinted 1971 by photo-lithography in the Republic of
Ireland for the Irish University Press, Shannon
T. M. MacGlinchey, Publisher
Robert Hogg, Printer
0 7165 1401 X

M 5/14/71
mgh 11/3/72